**MARGARET
PRESTON
RECENT
PAINTINGS
1929.**

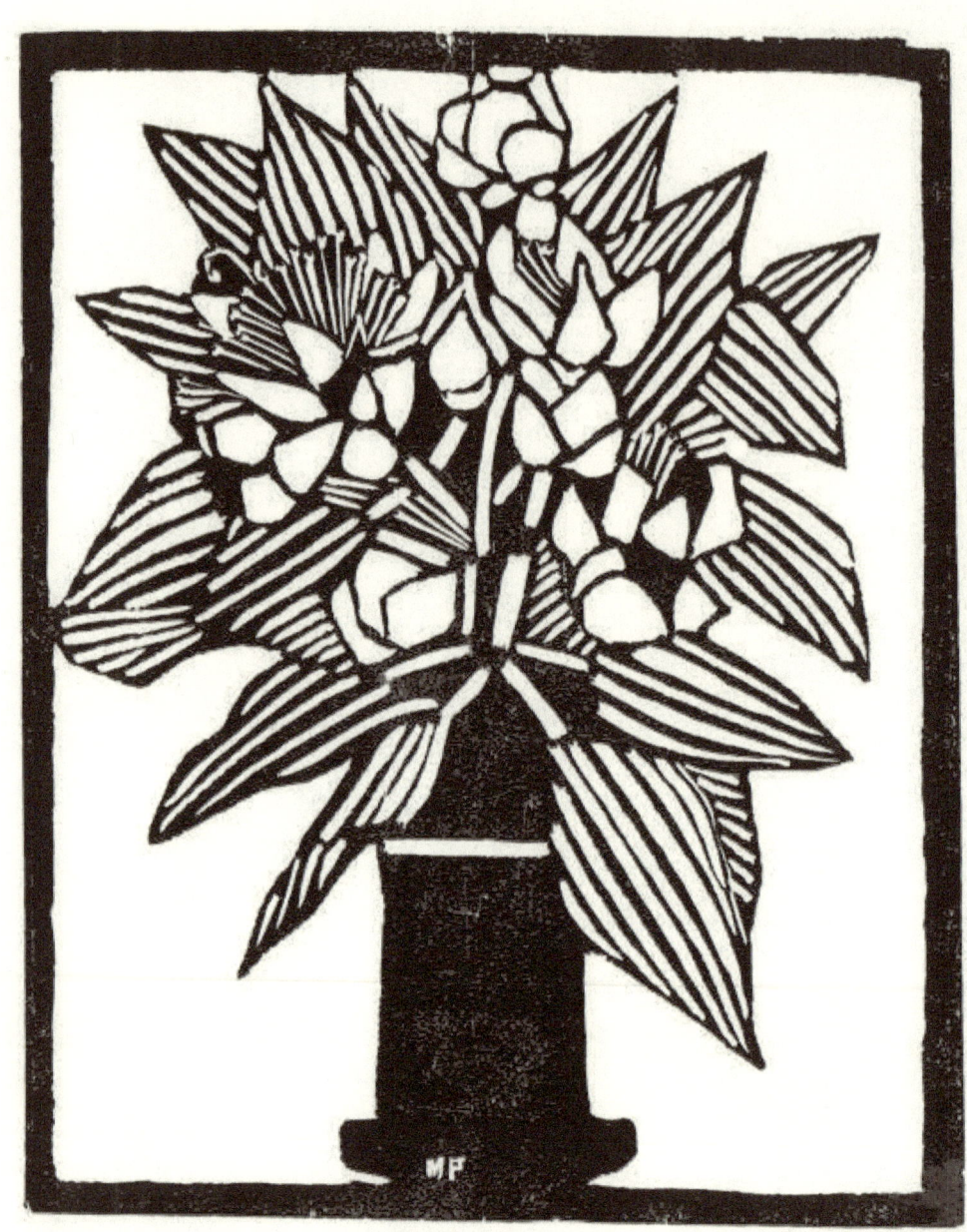

MARGARET PRESTON
RECENT PAINTINGS
1929

MARGARET PRESTON

RECENT PAINTINGS
1929

ART IN AUSTRALIA LTD.
24 BOND STREET • SYDNEY

**THIS EDITION IS LIMITED
TO 250 COPIES, OF WHICH
THIS IS NUMBER**

LIST of PLATES

Special Plate—Original Coloured Woodcut Printed and Coloured by Margaret Preston

WOODCUTS

	COVER DESIGN
West Australian Banksia	PLATE 1
Everlasting Flowers	PLATE 2
W.A. Native Flowers	PLATE 3
Flannel Flowers	PLATE 4
Ti-Trees	PLATE 5
Jug of Flowers	PLATE 6
The Spit Bridge	PLATE 7
West Australian Gum Blossom	PLATE 8
Bowl of Roses	PLATE 9

The plates for this book were engraved by Messrs. Bacon & Company Ltd., of Crane Place Sydney, and the colour plates were printed by W. T. Baker Sydney, for the publishers: Art in Australia Ltd., 24 Bond St., Sydney, Australia

FOREWORD

THIS portfolio of exquisite reproductions may be taken as representing the latest phase in the artistic development of one who must be regarded as the most individualistic explorer in the regions of colour and pattern that Australia has ever produced It is only a few years now since the name of Margaret Preston startlingly revealed itself in the largest of capital letters. The first symptoms of her success were demonstrated by the sudden eagerness with which her fellow-craftsmen purchased and treasured her small output. It was as though they had been instantaneously blessed by revelation. Somebody had come among them speaking with a new and broader accent and they were astonished and enchanted by her speech. There is some distance between the appreciation of the artist-connoisseur and that of the average picture collector and the lapse of time between the first discernment of her genius and public applause was only to be expected. The subtleties of her particular idiom already are being vaguely approved by the many while the members of her growing band of ardent admirers, who perceive the finer intricacies of
[her

her intention, fight among themselves for the possession of her latest creation. Already her work is causing some stir abroad, a rare occurrence in the history of Australian art and those who have followed closely her development and considered the totality of her achievement at the present time cannot help but foresee that the paintings of Margaret Preston will be as avidly sought in the future as are those of Paul Gauguin in the art market of to-day

Sydney Ure Smith
Leon Gellert
Editors

92 APHORISMS by MARGARET PRESTON and OTHERS

1. AN aphorism is the product of the familiar earth and smacks of the world we live in

2. AN artist is something on two legs with a simple soul and a belief that he was made before God

3. THAT art is not imitation of nature is as old as most ills

4. ONE cannot teach art only point out a way for another to find it for himself

5. DON'T judge a picture by its title—nude gods and goddesses are only unclothed models

6. WORKS of art are causes of wonder inter est and admiration but a person who looks for beauty primarily in the arts cannot have

have loved nature and will never understand the piety of art

7 BEAUTY is not intrinsic in any form—it comes to make that form

8 HE who uses only the sight of the eyes is acted on by what he sees, it is the intuition of the spirit that gives the assurance of certainty

9 AMONG men reject none; among things reject nothing. This is called comprehensive criticism

10 THERE are many woolly substitutes for thought

11 PAINTING is a personal matter; it should be judged from the point of view of the artist

12 ALL art whether it be good or bad is expressing the artist's personality to some degree

13 IT is not possible to understand without surrender. As long as the slightest inclination to criticism remains in the consciousness it is hopeless to do justice to what is strange

14 HARDNESS of training ultimately makes wise even the fool

15 NO-ONE is ever too old to know better

16 REALISM is the line of least resistance

17 ART was developed before religion. The native carved the stick then worshipped it

18 ART like life is either growing or going

19 THE Law of Life is of a fiendish, not of a divine kind; modern art accepts this truth

20 A drawing need not appear to be the work of an academician; it passes by rights of its own

21 PURE form is an artistic reality, it is not imitative

22 BAD art gives the feeling of satiation with fulfilment

23 THE imitative artist contemplates all creative powers as the eunuchs contemplated Don Juan as he passed through hell on the White Horse

24 MODERN art is attached to science. The world that science is making may be disgusting but it is the world in which we have to live and it condemns to futility all who are too blind to notice it

25 ONCE design enters, every form or shape realized on the canvas alters the nature and character of the original stimulus

26 LINES, masses of forms, have a life of their own which is nearly always at variance with natural appearance

27 ART is a problem of relationships

28 LINE specifies the general mass or planes functioning in a design

29 ARTISTS who are subservient to the physical beauties of their models produce only a high form of illustration

30 THE slogan for modern art is "Mind before Matter" but the slogan for ancestral art is "Matter before Mind" or what was good enough for daddy is good enough for me

31 IN art a young student should be ultra-modern or ultra-ancestral. There should be no happy medium for youth

32 LIVE in harmony with your age

33 THE great problem of the present generation in art is to get over the idea that art is imitation of nature

34 THE work of a generation is not really understood before the coming of the generation which follows

35 THE easiest way to understand modern art is to buy an example and live with it. Custom makes consciousness

36 **TO** Critics: Write of the quick, as you do of the dead, with the same detachment

37 **BETTER** belong to the Good-byes than work to be a "Good buy"

38 **AN** aesthetic object is authentic if at any moment it is actually perceived as such

39 **EVERY** aesthetic expression is dynamic and therefore involves distortion

40 **WHAT** else can be said of ancestral art: what is being done now can only have been done better or worse

41 **THE** dower of ignorance is to distrust all that it cannot feel

42 **FISH** swim in a pathless medium yet they habitually swim in schools

43 **AESTHETIC** values are essentially individual and occasional, the greatness of master pieces remains purely nominal until intuition in somebody recognises it and confirms it

44 **BEFORE** children can conspire in inventing and playing a game they must be born contemporary brats

45 **MODERN** Art, to survive, must be made necessary to modern society. The first step is to find subjects that can symbolize what is to

us

us the meaning of our world as effectively as the religious pictures once did for other times

46 WHY there are so many tables of still life in modern paintings is because they are really laboratory tables on which aesthetic problems can be isolated

47 ASK the normal intelligent healthy boy of today to define "civilization"—he answers at once "aeroplanes"

48 THE ways of unimaginative men are singularly fierce

49 TOO much craft in art ruins the art in the craft

50 CONTEMPORARY art is the connoisseur's comfort and the critic's curse

51 THE Chu and Chin periods originated the sect of "The Company of Lofty Talkers"; it died out in the same period

52 TO be natural in art is to be sincere

53 A lemon can be an inspiration as well as a fruit

54 IF painting is based on realism a long continuation is not possible

55 KNOWLEDGE is not truth; truth is temperament; with some people lying is an art with others it is a pastime

56 **C**OLOUR is an extravagance of the mind
Colour is the emblem of change

57 **T**HE past is ours, but, what's far more, the future can be provided for

58 **D**O not learn too long. Art that is learned is only second-hand

59 **T**HE act of painting involves the acceptance of an artificial expedient for producing on a flat surface in two dimensions the similitude of something that exists in three. So art must be from the brain

60 **M**ODERN work draws its sustenance from life; ancestral art from the imitation of pictures of the past

61 **A**N artist's evolution should always be in relation to himself and independent of outside forces

62 **A**RT is the autobiography of each individual artist

63 **A**NY subject that engrosses the artist and sets his creative faculties in motion is an adequate subject

64 **O**NE can live for years with nothing on outside but only a few hours with nothing in inside; this applies to art also

65 IMITATORS serve only to emphasise the greatness of their master

66 DOMINION art suffers from lack of exploration

67 ONE group of cubists loves structure, such as those who love the definite cubic element in a tree, in a landscape, a human body, in the firmness of its cubic anatomy, and the other line of cubism leads away from reality to spiritual expression; it follows the inner lead of any natural object through a maze of angles and balanced lines; it searches for the inner meaning of natural objects

68 TO be lucid, to know of what one is capable is the first thing of importance for the artist

69 THE Heian period (Japanese) invented tasteful patterns on a fancy paper for writing poems

70 IN the Toyotomi era (Japanese) art attained a position of unparalleled glory as it then came to be employed by the military class as a medium for displaying their pomp and power

71 MICHAEL Angelo designed the costumes for the attendants at the Vatican, which same design is worn at the present day

72 NEVER try to return to nature; nature never stands still

73 ART is universal enough to contain all appeals

74 DECORATION without ornamentation Enough or too much

75 AN epilogue: "His collection of art was a portrait of himself"

76 EVERY city should have a "Juryfree" exhibition once a year

77 ANECDOTE: One day at Theophile Gautier's Baudelaire saw his friend Charles Asselineau handling a hideous little Congo idol carved from the wood of a fig tree; it was the figure of a man with a head twice the size of the body and a mouth stretching from ear to ear "What a dreadful looking thing," exclaimed Asselineau, putting it down in disgust "Take care" said Baudelaire, "Suppose it were the true God"

78 SOME Chinese critics hold that topographical conditions influence art; that if men are born in a temperate climate with mild and graceful scenery, they are liable to become either genteel or refined, or light-hearted and hypocritical; on the other hand those reared amongst mountains and grand scenery become manly and powerful, also rude and unbridled—this is idealism

79 A collection of bad art is dead; it can only speak to you of prices and auctions

A collection of true art is in a way a confession one once more becomes acquainted with the artist

80 A second anecdote: It is said that in Greece paintings of dishes heaped with fruits and viands, which were known as "Xenia" or "guest pictures" were to be found in most households; when the customary hospitality was partaken of by a guest with an exaggerated appetite he was advised to apply himself to the picture for his further satisfaction

81 BE square without being angular

82 THERE is no superiority in art

83 WE must expect the arts to remain in the hands of traditional artists, but these artists lose nothing by occasionally joining in an aesthetic experiment, even if only for a holiday

84 THE masses will always remain external

85 THERE are masters of art and art masters

86 CUBISM and nature are only relative

87 TRUE balance can only be found in a freedom which permits of knowing all—and taking the consequences

88 ONE of the reasons why painters avoid mak
[ing

ing their works too close to nature is a desire to leave room for the exercise of the imaginative powers on the part of those who examine their works

89 ART, to fulfil its destiny, requires to be accepted by a nation or race and not by a few only

90 ART never improves, only changes

91 THE cultured man directs his energies inwards, the civilized man outwards

92 THE crux of the matter lies in self; unless we can get to the point of seeing that selves are not WE, but only us—that WE defend the past at the expense of the future, that WE defend our possessions at the expense of creative effort and so WE defend our mistakes

MARGARET PRESTON WOODCUTS

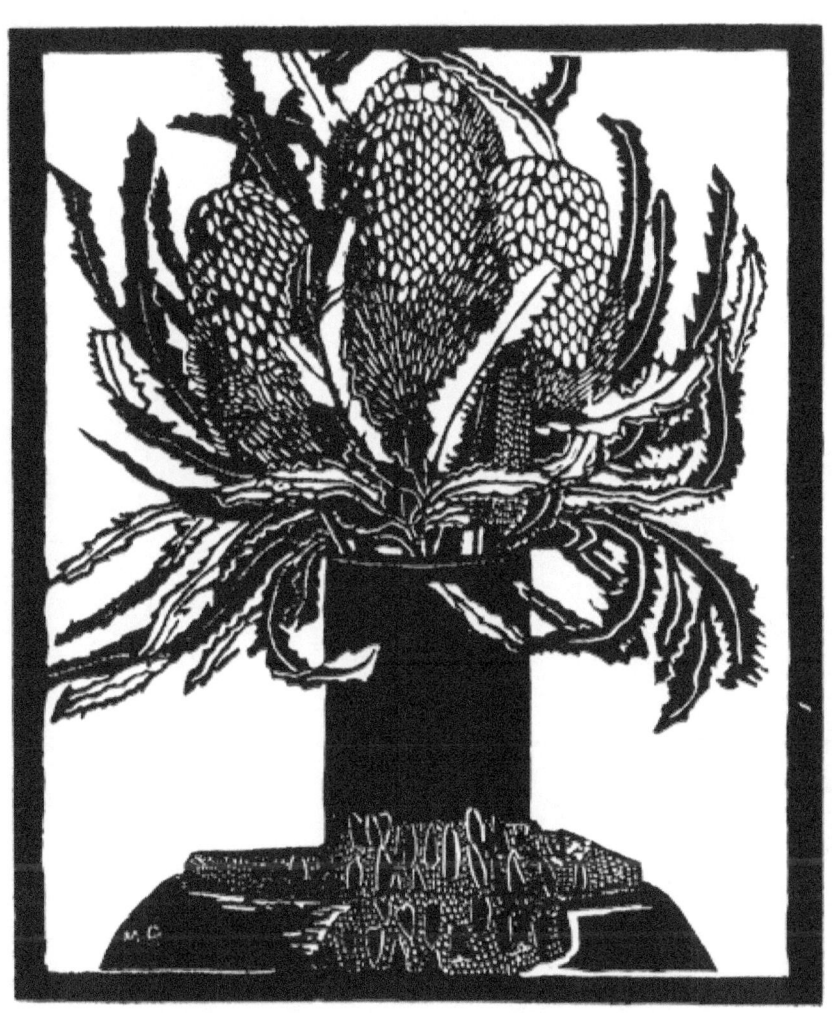

PLATE 1
West Australian Banksia

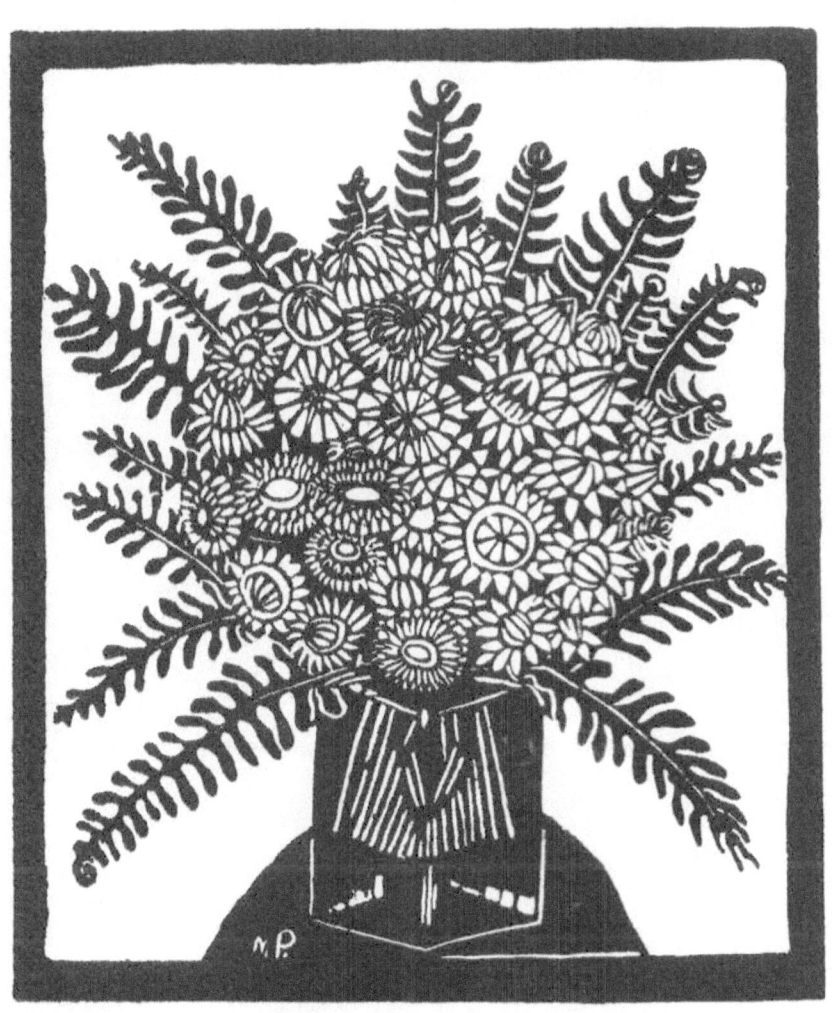

PLATE 2
Everlasting Flowers

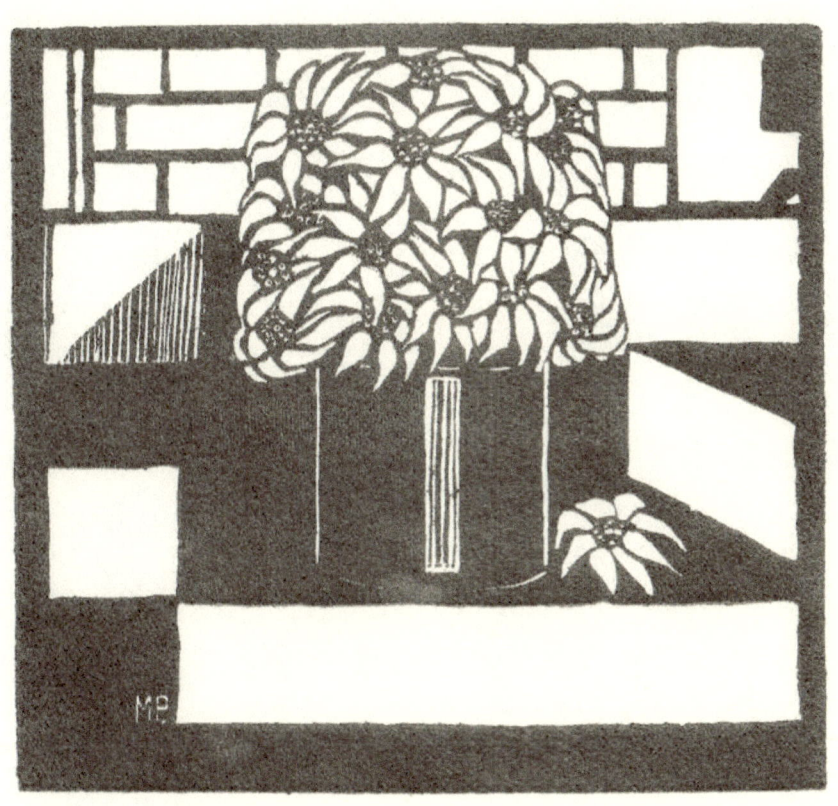

PLATE 4
Flannel Flowers

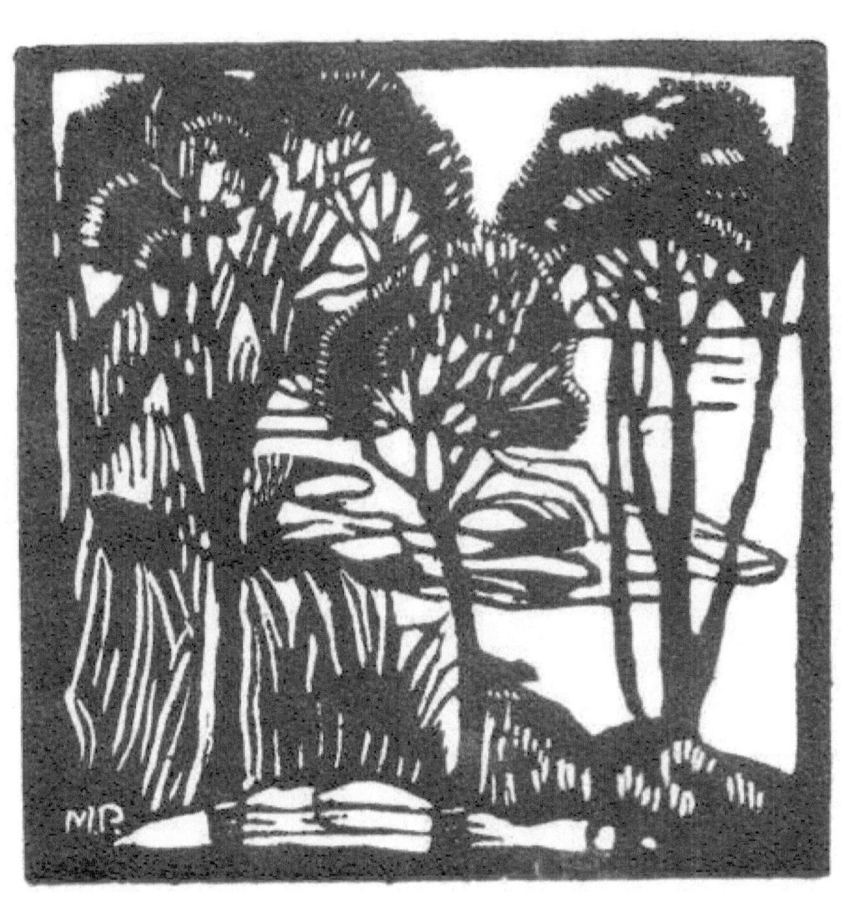

PLATE 5
Ti-Trees

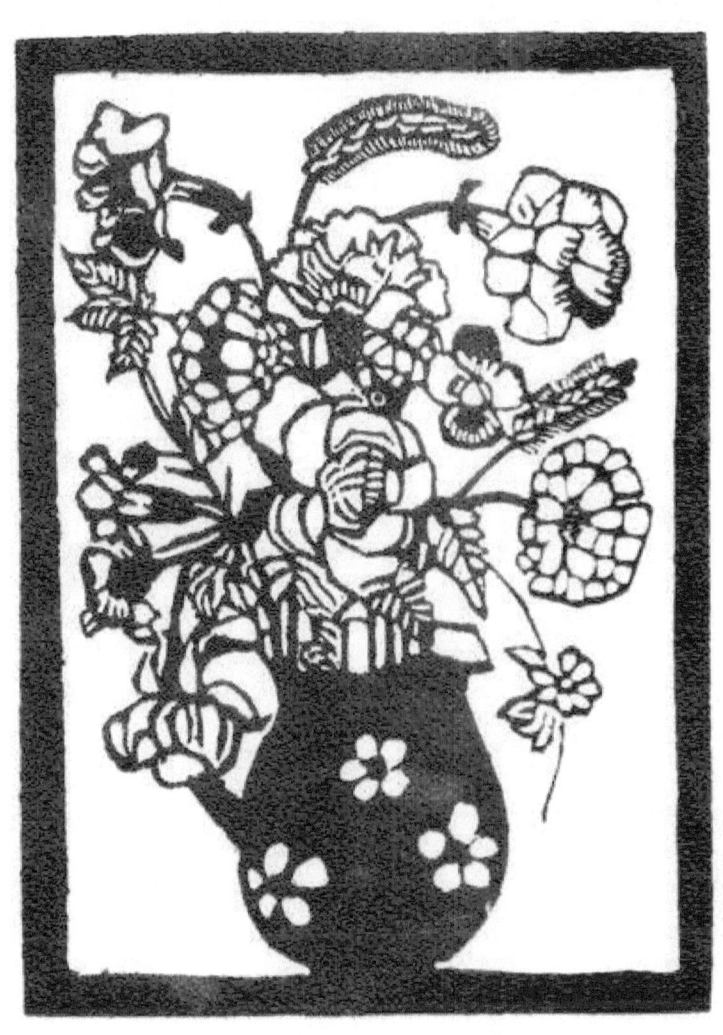

PLATE 6
Jug of Flowers

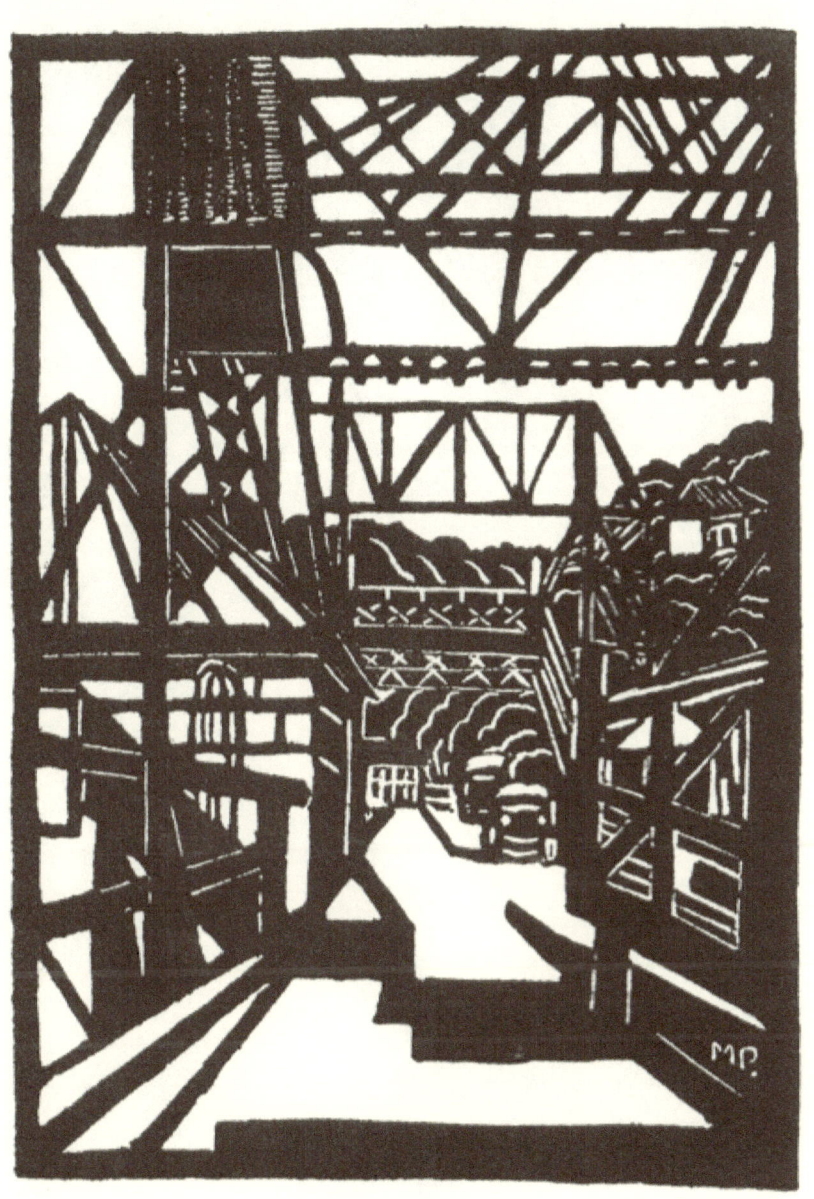

PLATE 7
The Spit Bridge

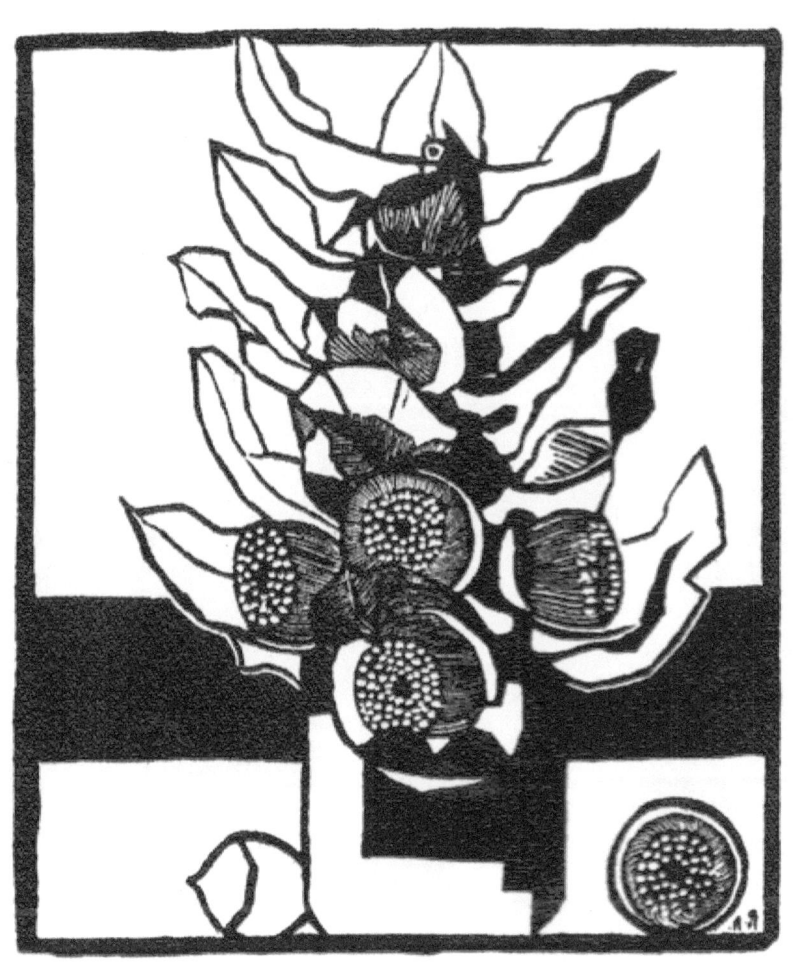

PLATE 8
West Australian Gum Blossom

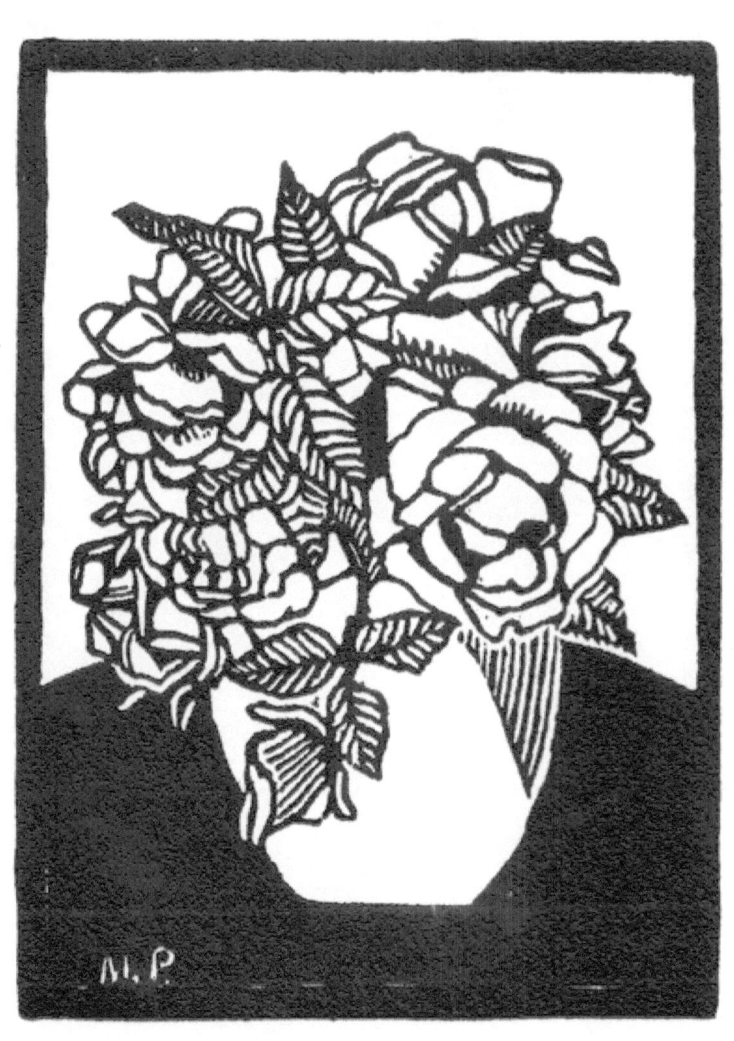

PLATE 9
Bowl of Roses

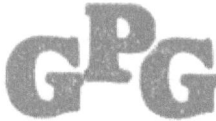

Typography & printing by Percy G. Green at Green Press, Franklin Street, Glebe, Sydney November, nineteen hundred & twenty-nine

This edition published by ETT Imprint, Exile Bay 2017

ETT IMPRINT
PO Box R1906
Royal Exchange NSW 1225
Australia

This book is copyright. Apart from any fair dealing for the purposes of private study, research, criticism or review, as permitted under the Copyright Act, no part may be reproduced by any process without written permission. Inquiries should be addressed to the publishers

Aphorisms first published by Art In Australia within Recent Paintings 1929

Extracts first published in Margaret Preston by Elizabeth Butel, 1985

This edition copyright © ETT Imprint, 2017. Reprinted 2017

ISBN 978-1-925706-18-5 (paper)

ISBN 978-1-925416-77-0 (ebook)

The author is grateful to the Trustee of the Estate Late Margaret Preston, the Permanent Trustee Company Limited, for permission to reproduce the images and writings of Margaret Preston in all editions

Design by Hanna Gotlieb

THIS BOOK IS AN INVESTMENT

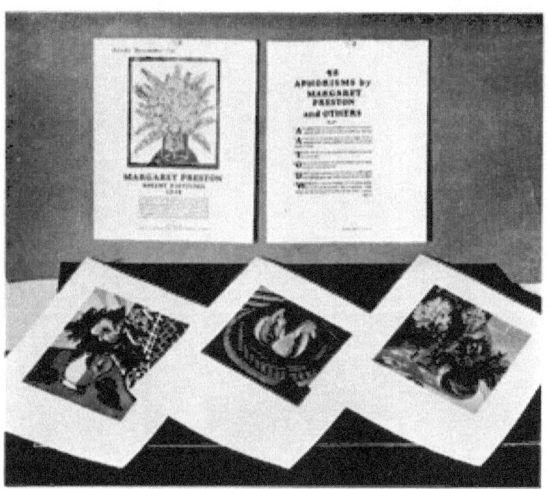

MARGARET PRESTON
RECENT PAINTINGS 1929

A portfolio bound in white linen containing 14 large colour plates, and also a book of aphorisms accompanied by reproductions of woodcuts. The portfolio also includes an original woodcut printed and coloured by the artist. Limited to 250 copies. Size of portfolio, 11 ins. x 13 ins.

PRICE **£5/5/-**

A duplicate set of colour prints for framing is in each portfolio.

PUBLISHED BY ART IN AUSTRALIA LTD.
24 BOND STREET, SYDNEY

www.ingramcontent.com/pod-product-compliance
Lightning Source LLC
Chambersburg PA
CBHW031513210526
45464CB00007B/2895